CW01220746

# HOMEWORK ACTIVITIES

# FRENCH

YEAR

3

Rising Stars UK Ltd.
7 Hatchers Mews, Bermondsey Street, London SE1 3GS
www.risingstars-uk.com

All facts are correct at time of going to press.

First published in 2008 as Euro Stars Primary French Stage 1.
This revised edition published 2011.
Text, design and layout © Rising Stars UK Ltd.

Copymaster content: Marie-Thérèse Bougard
Cover design: Words & Pictures Ltd
Design: Redmoor Design / Glen Keegan
Publisher: Nathalie Morris
Editorial: Pat Dunn
Illustrations: David Woodroffe

**British Library Cataloguing in Publication Data**
A CIP record for this book is available from the British Library.

ISBN: 978-1-84680-936-1

Printed by: Newnorth Print Ltd.

# Contents

# Introduction

*Rising Stars Homework Activities French* is an updated series of photocopiable activities offering a ready-made solution for homework or classwork. They have been written so that no preparation is required – simply photocopy and go! The activities can be used alongside all your other teaching resources and are ideal for homework or extra practice in class.

## Copymasters

The copymasters support teaching of the *Key Stage 2 Scheme of Work for French* and the *Key Stage 2 Framework for Languages*. Six copymasters are provided per Scheme of Work unit, for practice and reinforcement, with clear instructions in English to support pupils. One copymaster in each set of six focuses on pronunciation.

## Integrating French into your teaching

From the outset, try to use French as much as possible for routine classroom communication. It is important that children, even at the very early stages of language learning, begin to see French as a real means of communication and not just as a subject that they learn at school. Try to encourage them to use French themselves with each other e.g. when playing games: *C'est à toi!* (It's your turn!), as well as when speaking to you: *Oui, monsieur/madame!* (Yes, sir/miss!).

To support children in this, spend some time at the beginning of each year introducing and reinforcing useful classroom phrases and simple instructions, e.g. *Regardez, Écoutez, Bravo*. Continue to reinforce them throughout each year. Involve children when devising mimes to represent classroom instructions, and practise them using the French version of Simon Says (*Jacques a dit*). You could also begin a classroom display of useful phrases, with symbols or icons representing the meanings, e.g. a pair of eyes for *Regardez*. Add to the display throughout the year as new phrases crop up.

## Links with a French partner school

Ideally, set up a link with a partner school in a French-speaking country and keep in touch via email, blog, etc. This can provide an invaluable ongoing source of cultural information and authentic material for projects, surveys, etc. The British Council manages a website called Global Gateway (www.globalgateway.org.uk) to help schools set up international links.

A partner school in a French-speaking country can provide you with a source of real French resources, e.g. food packaging, magazines, posters, postcards, bus and train tickets, shop receipts, menus. Any small everyday item that provides a snapshot of everyday life in France, or a French-speaking country, is useful. Your own pupils can return the favour by collecting similar items to send to their counterparts in other countries.

It is also important for your pupils to hear real French spoken in everyday situations. Try to provide opportunities for them to experience authentic audio-visual content, e.g. CDs, DVDs, videos and real-time online material.

### Songs and Rhymes

Sing along to a classic French song or rhyme to immerse all children in the language. This is a really fun way to engage *all* learners and encourage them to get to grips with French culture.

# Copymaster answers

**Copymaster 1**
*No answers*

**Copymaster 2**
*Top picture*: Tu t'appelles comment?
*Bottom picture*: Ça va mal.

**Copymaster 3**
Bonjour!; Au revoir!; trois; quatre

**Copymaster 4**
bonjour – au revoir; bien – mal; oui – non; un – deux

**Copymaster 5**
1 un; 2 deux; 3 trois; 4 quatre; 5 cinq; 6 six; 7 sept; 8 huit;
9 neuf; 10 dix

**Copymaster 6**
mon frère; ma mère; mon père

**Copymaster 7**
11 onze; 12 douze; 13 treize; 14 quatorze; 15 quinze;
16 seize; 17 dix-sept; 18 dix-huit; 19 dix-neuf; 20 vingt

**Copymaster 8**
*Top list*: marron; *Middle list*: dix-huit; *Bottom list*: dix-sept

**Copymaster 9**
le chat; quatre; Cache-cache

**Copymaster 10**
*Top picture*: Je préfère le football.
*Bottom picture*: Je préfère Cache-cache.

**Copymaster 11**
*Top picture:* J'ai trois chiens.
*Bottom picture:* Je préfère le saut à la corde.

**Copymaster 12**
le football – *football;* les marrons – *conkers;*
le Chat Perché – *tag;* le Cache-cache – *hide and seek*

**Copymaster 13**
*Children's personal response*

**Copymaster 14**
*Top picture*: Je lis. *Bottom picture*: Je danse.

**Copymaster 15**
janvier; Je chante; Je danse.

**Copymaster 16**
*Series 1*: mars; *Series 2*: juin; *Series 3*: décembre

**Copymaster 17**
*Top list:* je lis; *Middle list:* ça va mal;
*Bottom list:* joyeux anniversaire

**Copymaster 18**
Je lance le ballon. – *I throw the ball.*
Je lis. – *I read.*

**Copymaster 19**
*The numbered areas of the picture should be coloured as follows:*
1 *red*; 2 *blue*; 3 *yellow*; 4 *purple*; 5 *green*; 6 *orange*; 7 *brown*;
8 *black*; 9 *white*

**Copymaster 20**
les cheveux – *hair*; les yeux – *eyes*; le nez – *nose*;
la bouche – *mouth*; le bras – *arm*; la jambe – *leg*

**Copymaster 21**
deux yeux bleus; les cheveux

**Copymaster 22**
*blue* – bleu; *yellow* – jaune; *red* – rouge; *green* – vert;
*purple* – violet; *black* – noir

**Copymaster 23**
*She has a red mouth, blue eyes and black hair.*

**Copymaster 24**
*blue + yellow = green; red + green = brown;*
*red + white = pink; black + white = grey*

**Copymaster 25**
*The correct pictures are:*
*Top*: horse; *Bottom*: mouse

**Copymaster 26**
la souris – *mouse*; le lapin – *rabbit*; le cheval – *horse*;
la pomme – *apple*; le mouton – *sheep*

**Copymaster 27**
douze souris rouges

**Copymaster 28**
Lutin – *rabbit*; Mimi – *mouse*; Hannibal – *horse*; Tintin – *dog*;
*the cat's name isn't known*

**Copymaster 29**
Il galope. – *It gallops.*; Il sautille. – *It hops.*; Elle trottine. –
*It scurries.;* Il court. – *It runs.*

**Copymaster 30**
*Top list:* la pomme; *Middle list:* le chapeau; *Bottom list:* gris

**Copymaster 31**
un concombre – *cucumber*; du cresson – *watercress*;
un haricot – *bean*; une laitue – *lettuce*; un marché – *market*;
une tomate – *tomato*

**Copymaster 32**
*Children's personal response*

**Copymaster 33**
Bonjour!; onze; le concombre

**Copymaster 34**
*Across: market* – marché; *watercress* – cresson;
*lettuce* – laitue; *tomato* – tomate
*Down: bean* – haricot; *cucumber* – concombre

**Copymaster 35**
*Top picture*: Je n'aime pas les tomates.
*Bottom picture*: J'aime le cresson.

**Copymaster 36**
*Children's personal response*

# Moi (All about me)

**Colour in the French words under each picture. Then say each word aloud.**

Bonjour!

Au revoir!

# **Moi** (All about me)

**Choose the correct sentence for each picture. Then say the sentence aloud.**

Un, deux, trois …

Tu t'appelles comment?

Bonjour.

Ça va mal.

## **Moi** (All about me)

**The letter 'r' is missing from each word. Complete each word, then say it aloud.**

r

Bonjou_!

Au _evoi_!

**3**

t_ois

**4**

quat_e

Rising Stars Homework Activities: French Year 3 Copymaster 3 © Rising Stars UK Ltd. 2011

# Moi (All about me)

**Use the words at the bottom of the page to complete the pairs.**

bonjour ___ ___ _ _ _ _ _ _

bien ___ _ _

oui ___ _ _

un ___ _ _ _

deux      non      mal      au revoir

Name _____  Date _____

# Moi (All about me)

**Draw lines to link each word to the correct number.**

un                    4

deux                  1

trois                 10

quatre                2

cinq                  7

six                   9

sept                  5

huit                  6

neuf                  8

dix                   3

Name _____ Date _____

## Moi (All about me)

The letters 'ère' are missing from each word. Complete each word, then say it aloud.

mon fr____

ma m____

mon p____

# Jeux et chansons
## (Games and songs)

**Draw lines to link each word to the correct number.**

onze            20

douze           11

treize          14

quatorze        12

quinze          17

seize           13

dix-sept        15

dix-huit        16

dix-neuf        18

vingt           19

# Jeux et chansons
## (Games and songs)

**Cross out the odd one out from each list.**

douze
treize
marron

Cache-cache
dix-huit
football

dix-sept
le chat
la souris

Name _____ Date _____

# Jeux et chansons
## (Games and songs)

**The letter 'a' is missing from each word.**
**Complete each word, then say it aloud.**

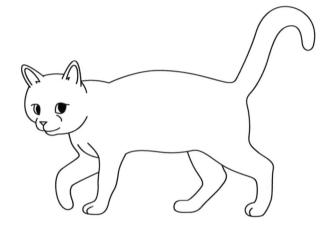

le ch_t

**4**

qu_tre

C_che-c_che

Name _____ Date _____

# Jeux et chansons
## (Games and songs)

**Colour in the picture of your favourite game. Then copy the correct label under it.**

---

---

Je préfère Cache-cache.        Je préfère le football.

**Jeux et chansons**
(Games and songs)

**Choose the correct sentence for each picture. Then say the sentence aloud.**

J'ai trois chiens.

J'ai trois chats.

Je préfère le football.

Je préfère le saut à la corde.

# Jeux et chansons
## (Games and songs)

**Draw lines to link each French word to the correct picture.**

le football

les marrons

le Chat Perché

le Cache-cache

# On fait la fête (Celebrations)

**Find your favourite two months in the list and colour them.**

janvier

février

mars

avril

mai

juin

juillet

août

septembre

octobre

novembre

décembre

Name _____ Date _____

# On fait la fête (Celebrations)

**Circle the correct sentence for each picture, then say it aloud.**

Je saute.

Je lis.

Je lance le ballon.

Je danse.

Name _____ Date _____

# On fait la fête (Celebrations)

The letters 'an' are missing from each word. Complete each word, then say it aloud.

j _ _ vier

Je ch _ _ te.

Je d _ _ se.

Rising Stars Homework Activities: French Year 3 Copymaster 15 © Rising Stars UK Ltd. 2011

Name _____ Date _____

# On fait la fête (Celebrations)

**Complete the series, then say the words aloud.**

janvier

février

_ _ _ _

avril

mai

_ _ _ _

juillet

août

septembre

octobre

novembre

_ _ _ _ _ _ _ _

juin

décembre

mars

# On fait la fête (Celebrations)

## Cross out the odd one out from each list.

je nage
je saute
je lis

super
chouette
ça va mal

joyeux anniversaire
janvier
juin

# On fait la fête (Celebrations)

**Read the caption and draw the action.**

Je lance le ballon.

Je lis.

Name _____ Date _____

**Match the numbers with the colours to colour the picture.**

**1** rouge        **4** violet        **7** marron

**2** bleu         **5** vert          **8** noir

**3** jaune        **6** orange        **9** blanc

Name _____  Date _____

# **Portraits** (Portraits)

**Draw a line from each label to the correct part of the picture. Then say the words out loud.**

les cheveux        les yeux

le nez

la bouche

le bras

la jambe

# **Portraits** (Portraits)

**The letters 'eu' are missing from these labels. Complete the words, then say them aloud.**

eu

d_ _x  y_ _x  bl_ _s

les chev_ _x

**Portraits** (Portraits)

## Find six colours in the grid, and copy them out.

| v | b | l | e | u | r |
|---|---|---|---|---|---|
| i | i | s | i | n | j |
| o | v | e | r | t | a |
| l | s | t | a | r | u |
| e | n | o | i | r | n |
| t | r | o | u | g | e |

blue _____

yellow _____

red _____

green _____

purple _____

black _____

# Portraits (Portraits)

**Draw a face which matches this description.**

Elle a la bouche rouge, les yeux bleus et
les cheveux noirs.

Rising Stars Homework Activities: French Year 3 Copymaster 23 © Rising Stars UK Ltd. 2011

# Portraits (Portraits)

**Colour in these words in the correct colour.**

bleu + jaune = vert

rouge + vert = marron

rouge + blanc = rose

noir + blanc = gris

# Les quatre amis
## (The four friends)

**Colour in the right animal in each picture.**

le cheval

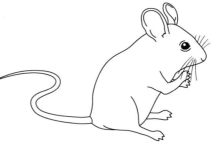

la souris

Name _____  Date _____

# Les quatre amis
## (The four friends)

**Draw a line from each label to the correct part of the picture. Then trace the words and say them out loud.**

la souris

la pomme

le lapin

le mouton

le cheval

# Les quatre amis
## (The four friends)

The letters 'ou' are missing from these words. Complete them, and say the phrase aloud. Then colour the picture.

ou

d_ _ze   s_ _ris   r_ _ges

# Les quatre amis
## (The four friends)

**Read the rhyme, and circle the words you recognise. Then draw lines to match the names of the animals to the pictures.**

Le lapin s'appelle Lutin

Et la souris s'appelle Mimi.

Le cheval s'appelle Hannibal

Et le chien s'appelle Tintin.

Et le chat?

Je ne sais pas!

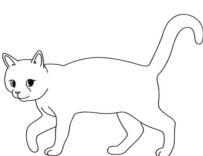

Name _____ Date _____

# Les quatre amis
## (The four friends)

**Draw lines to link each French sentence to the correct picture.**

Il galope.

Il sautille.

Elle trottine.

Il court.

Rising Stars Homework Activities: French Year 3 Copymaster 29 © Rising Stars UK Ltd. 2011

Name _____ Date _____

# Les quatre amis
(The four friends)

**Cross out the odd one out from each list.**

le cheval
le mouton
la pomme

le chat
le chien
le chapeau

vite
lentement
gris

# Ça pousse! (Growing things)

**Draw lines to match the French words to the correct items.**

un concombre

du cresson

un haricot

une laitue

un marché

une tomate

| market |
| --- |

**bean**

**watercress**

**cucumber**

Name _____ Date _____

# Ça pousse! (Growing things)

**What do you like? Trace in green the words for the things you like.**

J'aime …

les concombres

les haricots

les laitues

les tomates

**What do you dislike? Trace in red the words for the things you dislike.**

Je n'aime pas …

les concombres

les haricots

les laitues

les tomates

# Ça pousse! (Growing things)

The letters 'on' are missing from each word. Complete each word, then say it aloud.

on

B_ _jour!

**11**

_ _ze

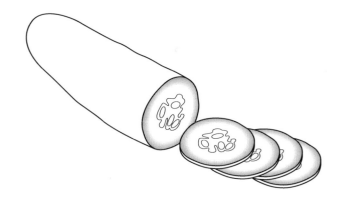

le c_ _combre

# Ça pousse! (Growing things)

**Look at the picture clues and complete the crossword grid.**

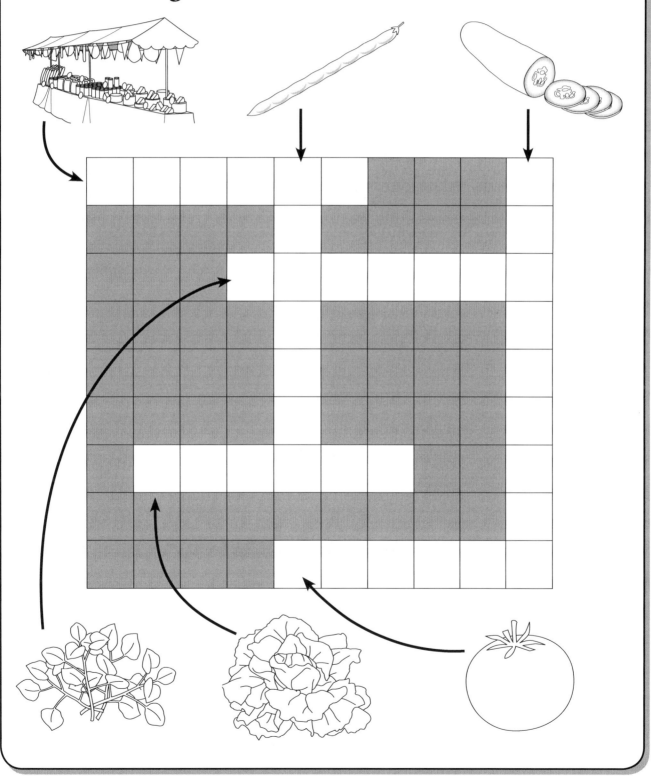

Name _____ Date _____

# Ça pousse! (Growing things)

**Circle the answer that matches the picture.**

Je n'aime pas les
concombres.

Je n'aime pas les tomates.

J'aime le cresson.

Je n'aime pas les laitues.

J'aime les tomates.

J'aime le cresson.

Rising Stars Homework Activities: French Year 3 Copymaster 35 © Rising Stars UK Ltd. 2011